Can You See Cat?

Written by Dee White

Illustrated by Tracie Grimwood

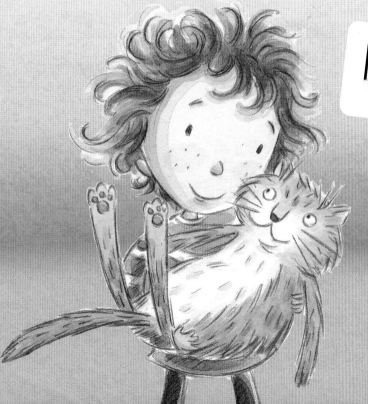

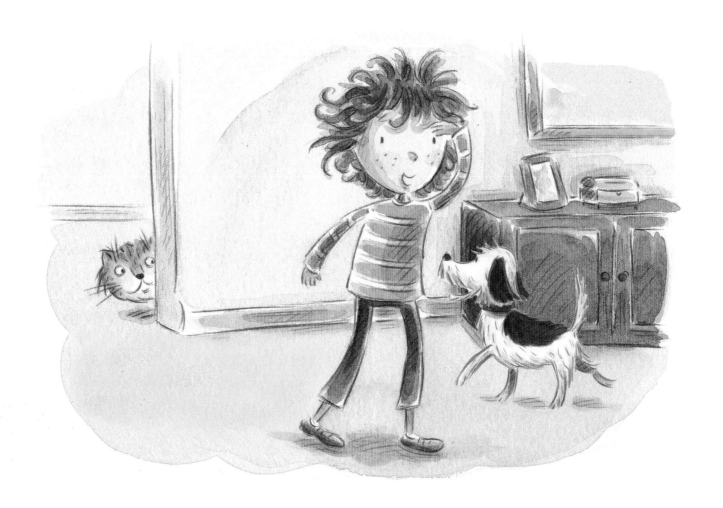

I can not see Cat.

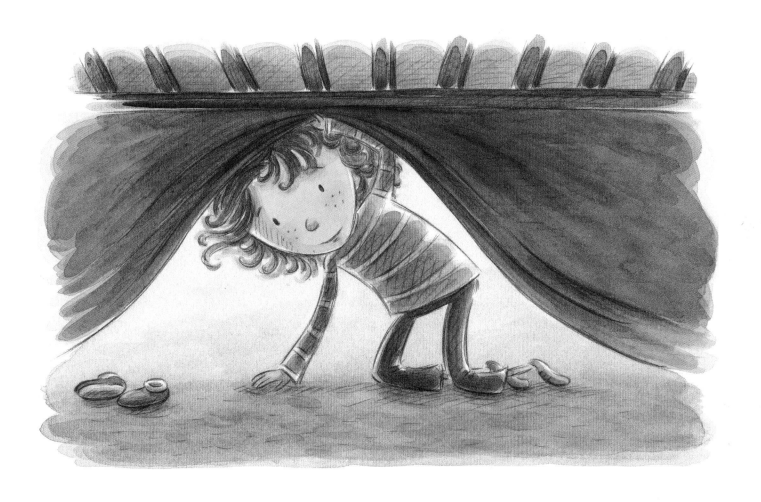

Is Cat under the bed? No!

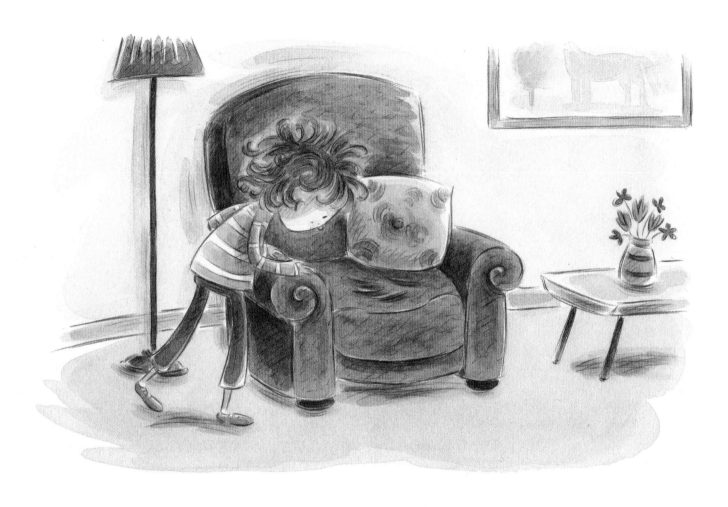

Is Cat on the chair? No!

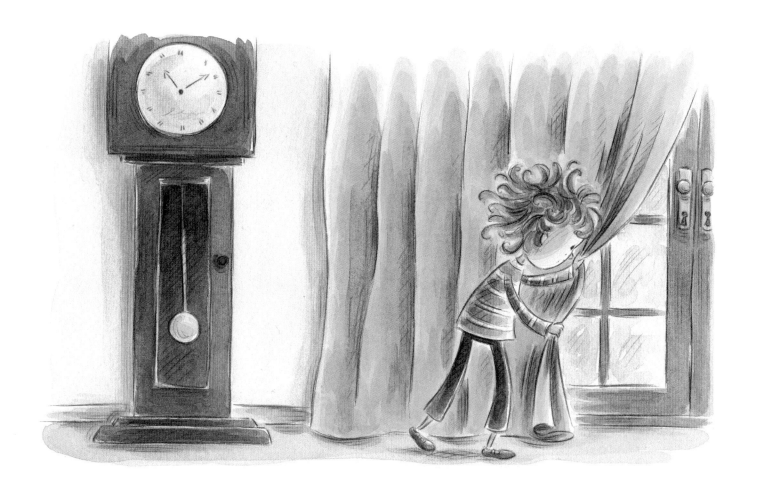

I can not see Cat.

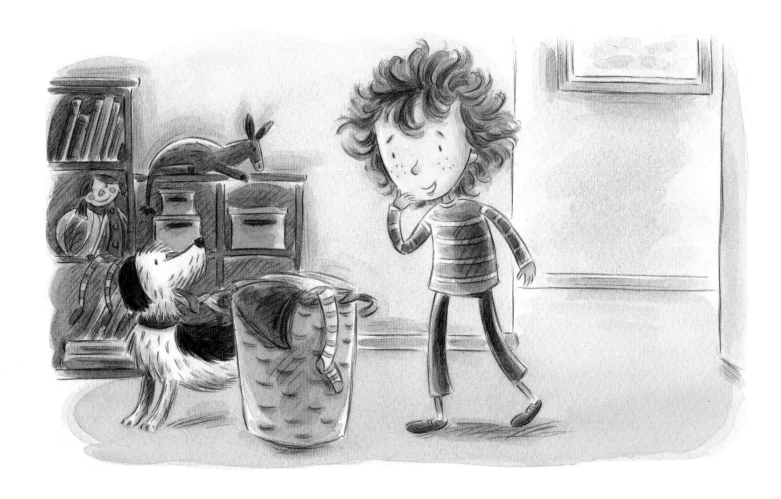

Is Cat in the basket?

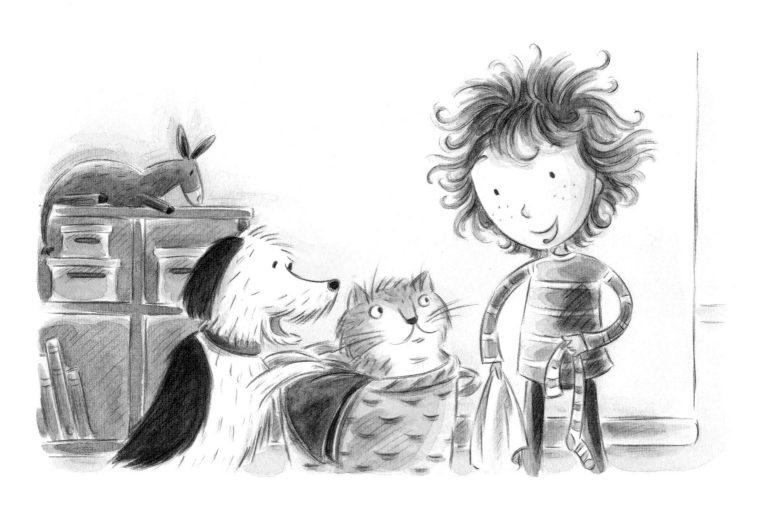

Cat is in the basket!

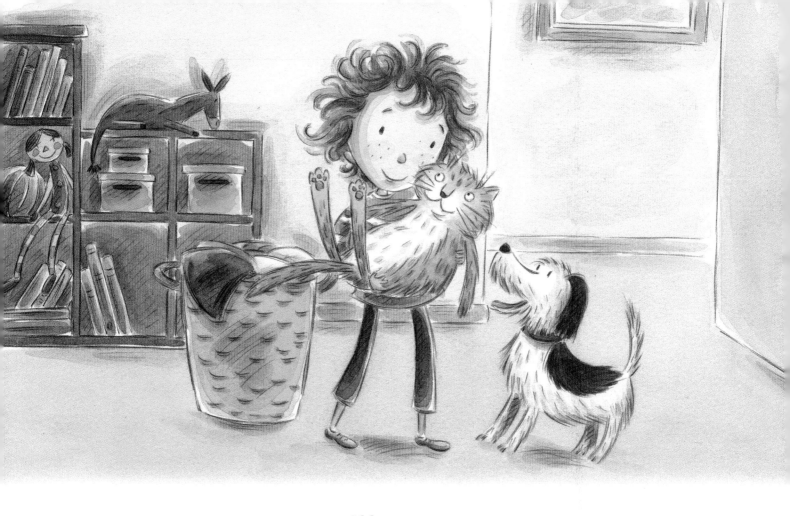

Silly Cat!